The
STUDENT-ATHLETE
PLAYBOOK

Success in the Classroom, Sports and Life!

Goals – Focus – Effort

The Student-Athlete Playbook
Success in the Classroom, Sports and Life!

breg1994.com   brownyouthsports.blogspot.com

makeawaynow.com   hustleuniversity.org

© 2014 Bar-Red Entertainment Group, LLC (BREG)

ISBN # 978-0692217979

Published By: BREG

Manufactured in the United States of America

First Printing, June 2014

The
STUDENT-ATHLETE
PLAYBOOK

Success in the Classroom, Sports and Life!

Written By:

Barry Brown

In <u>conjunction with:</u>

- ***Bar-Red Entertainment Group (BREG)***

- ***Hustle University (HU)***

- ***The "Make A Way" Education Program (MAW)***

BREG/HUSTLE U INC.
Atlanta   New York   Los Angeles

ACKNOWLEDGEMENTS:

Thanks be to God for the opportunity, ability, resources and determination to write this book!

I thank my mom, Lydia Arnold and my dad, Benjamin D. Brown for their constant belief in me, and for instilling tremendous values in me and my brother. Without their guidance, unconditional love and support, my life easily could have been much different. My mom has always encouraged me to be an owner, businessman and entrepreneur! My dad has always taught me how to conduct myself in business environments and to build and use my network of people to get business done the right way!

I thank my brother, Benjamin K. Brown for knowing how to relate to me and to provide that constant outlet for discussions and self-reflection that has helped me grow and mature as a man. I am very appreciative my brother!

I thank my smart, beautiful and strong wife, Tessa Brown! She is my rock and support base. She is my best friend, and the mother of my two amazing daughters (Amari & Aubri)! I love her and my daughters dearly! Here's a kiss for ya'll … Mmmuahhh!

Major love goes out to my entire family (Aunts, Uncles, Cousins, Nieces & Nephews) for their continuous love and support over the years!

I would like to thank these teachers and professors for challenging me and encouraging me in the classroom: Mrs. Smith (Fickett Elem.); Mrs. Ackey (Fickett Elem.); Ms. Bennett (Morrow Jr. High); Dr. Harris (Morrow High); Mrs. McDonald (Morrow High); Dr. Skinner (Presbyterian College); Dr. Ingram (Presbyterian College) and Dr. Stewart (Presbyterian College).

I would like to thank these coaches for being instrumental in my growth as a person and as an athlete: Coach Riley (Ben Hill/Sandtown Little League Football Programs); Coach Theodocian (Morrow High); Coach Creasman (Morrow High); Coach Moore (Morrow High); Coach Oswalt (Morrow High); Coach Householder (Morrow High); Coach Poss (Presbyterian College); Coach Huff (Presbyterian College); Coach Nichols (Presbyterian College); Coach Farrington (Presbyterian College) and Coach Whitt (Presbyterian College).

Shout out to my Morrow High School brothers: Cymande Bryant, Casey Gibson, Andre Hastings, Eric Atwater, Kenya "KP" Harrison, Rico Pittman, Eric Wilson, Tramon Rayner, Cornell "Fat" Hardy, Peady Hardy, Aaron Caldwell, Johnny Lawerence, Steve Reeves, Tron Evans, Carlos Head, Maurice Jackson & Dexter Phelps.

Shout out to my Presbyterian College brothers: Brad Jones, Eric Byrd, Rafael Traynum, Steve Gorrie, Duane Hagstrom, Mason Gordon, Kevin Smith, Quincy Eigner, DeAngelo Norris, Tony

"Blade" Robertson, Chris "Slim" Weldon, DeNorris "Peanut" Heard, Ivan Leaks, Corey Mckelvie, Bernard Vereen, Rodney Lightsey, Tyrone Phillips, Antonio Merriweather, Jeff Brown, Elton Pollock, Jr., Damond Carr, Lee Williamson and Robbie Kirk.

Thank you to my BREG Family: Tavares Stephens, Keeyen Martin, Magnem P.I., Lady X, Red Lo, Linden "L.A." Jackson, Edwin Wilson, Fatima Llashram, JaWar, Krucial R., Surreal, Spade Kosta, Thomas Swain, Mac Tee, Curry Jones, J.D. Fletcher, Jelani Whitest-Hill & Kirsten Fagin.

Thank you to my Hustle University/Make A Way Education Program family that encouraged me to write this book! Shout out to Hotep, Tierica Berry, Nicholas "Redd" Scott, Sr., Brandon Banks, Dr. Willie Jones, Dr. Pamela Bruening, Keysha Chester, Edward Morrow and Wess Walters.

Thank you to LaTashae "Tash" Walker, B. Elliot Hopkins (Director of Sports & Educational Services; National Federation of State High School Associations), Donnie Davis, Cool Water, Portia Jones and the high school student-athletes that took the time to contribute quotes for this book!

Thank you to my mentors/big brothers: Michael Sanders, Daryll Bowen (My Godfather), Silas "Si-Man" Alexander, Allen "The Music Specialist" Johnston and Rich Wilkins.

For those that I did not mention here, please know that I thank you very much for any contribution you have made to my life and this book.

One Love!

Table of Contents:

About the Author:

B. Brown is a native of Atlanta, GA, and he hails from SW Atlanta to be exact. He also claims Morrow, GA because his family moved to Clayton County, GA where he attended Morrow Junior High and Morrow Senior High.

He is a High School Graduate, former High School Two-Sport Athlete (Football & Baseball) and former Hip-Hop Artist/Rapper. He is a Registered Voter, a College Graduate, a former Collegiate Football Player, College Radio On-Air Personality and Assistant Student Manager of the College Radio Station at Presbyterian College (Clinton, SC). He is a Music Industry Executive/Consultant, Education Consultant, Motivational Speaker and Businessman. Last, but certainly not least, he is a Son, Brother, Nephew, Cousin, Husband, Father (Daddy) and Friend!

B. Brown encourages today's youth to make positive choices and to do positive things all the time. Each generation must be able to effectively articulate and communicate their thoughts, plans and ideas to others, while at the same time be able to effectively receive, analyze and over-stand information that is provided by others. As the saying goes, "Life is about choices, choose wisely."

"Your words, your dreams and your thoughts have power to create conditions in your life. What you speak about, you can bring about. Everything begins with your inner beliefs and belief in a higher standard." --- **B. Brown**

Introduction:

There are several reasons why I wrote this book, and I will touch on the main reasons during this introduction.

As far back as I can remember, my parents and everyone around me always expressed the importance of education. My relatives and friends of the family would always ask me and my brother how we were doing in school, and were we behaving well? I believed that was what adults were supposed to ask kids ... lol ...

When I was introduced to the first sport I ever played, it happened to be soccer. I don't remember asking to play, but I later found out from my mom that she signed me up to play soccer to improve the strength of my lungs. The old school way of saying it would be to "build up my wind." So I owe the beginning of my sports life to Dr. McGhee (Atlanta, GA) who advised my mom to get me involved in sports early on in life. Thank you mom, dad and Dr. McGhee!

As I grew older and was introduced to little league football at Ben Hill Recreation Center off of Campbellton Rd. in SW ATL, I believed football was the best thing since slice bread, and I was a natural! I was small, but I had no fear of hitting or being hit.

A year or two later I was introduced to baseball, and I liked it! But there was a snag. I was scared of the ball. To break my fear of the ball, the coaches put the catcher's equipment on me and had me play catcher. Would that be considered abuse in this day and time? ... Lol ... I don't know, but by the end of my first season of baseball, I made the All-Star team as a catcher! Great coaching and determination helped accomplish that result.

I would continue to play football and baseball all the way up to college where I would focus solely on football. I was given the opportunity to play baseball in college as well, but I decided to focus on my grades and education along with football instead of juggling education, football and baseball. Due to my physical size, maybe I should have focused on baseball and attempted to go pro; but hey, that's over with and I live a great life!

Looking back at my athletic career, I have a bunch of MVP (Most Valuable Player) trophies; a High School Baseball Player of the Year Award (County); a High School Football

State Championship; All-County & All-Region Awards; an Academic & Football Scholarship to attend college and a College Degree!!!

Yes, I'm good with those accomplishments because now I have a loving wife, two daughters and an amazing overall family!!!

So at the end of the day, I wrote this book to share with young people and adults alike that obtaining an education with marketable skills is the key ingredient to being a top-notch Student-Athlete. Using your mind in the classroom, on the field, court, track, etc. and in life will afford you opportunities that are truly beautiful!

Education and marketable skills unlock doors!!! Use your athletic prowess to secure the best education that you can secure; and never forget that your brain is your best physical asset as long as you are willing to develop it and strengthen it along with the rest of your body!

One Love!!!

What and who is a Student-Athlete?

*Definition of student (n) – Bing.com Dictionary

stu·dent

1. person studying: somebody who studies at a school, college, or university

2. knowledgeable or interested person: somebody who has studied or takes much interest in a particular subject

3. in training for job: studying as part of the training for a job or profession

*Definition of athlete (n) – Bing.com Dictionary

ath·lete

1. somebody with athletic ability; somebody with the abilities to participate in physical exercise, especially in competitive games and races

Student Athlete

From Wikipedia, the free encyclopedia

A **student athlete** (sometimes written **student–athlete**) is a participant in an organized competitive sport sponsored by the educational institution in which he or she is enrolled. Student athletes must typically balance the roles of being a full-time student and a full-time athlete.

My personal definition of **STUDENT-ATHLETE** is a person that takes their education and the opportunity to learn as serious as their athletics and the opportunity to develop as a top level athlete.

When you look at College Programs like the Hockey Team at Union College in New York, their 2014 NCAA Hockey National Championship Team boasted an awesome team G.P.A. of 3.9! Obviously, the college President, Athletic Director, Head Coach, Assistant Coaches and Players bought into the idea of excellence on and off of the ice! These young men are STUDENT-ATHLETES!!! Union College, I salute you!

Play #1: The Mindset

*Definition of mindset (n) – Bing.com Dictionary

mind·set

1. beliefs that affect somebody's attitude: a set of beliefs or a way of thinking that determine somebody's behavior and outlook

Everything, I mean everything begins with your thoughts, ideas and belief system. If you have tried a sport and had some moderate success, you may believe you have a future in that sport. Now, if you have tried a sport and it's just not your cup of tea, then you most likely will stop participating. Do you believe this is true in the majority of these types of situations around the world?

Let's look at the education side of this equation. I have met and/or observed a lot of adults and young people that just do not like being in school and learning. They are not interested in obtaining an education at all. For whatever reason, they do not develop the skills to function at a high level academically. By the time they reach high school, they have been socially passed on to the next grade consistently. This has nothing to do with intelligence. It has everything to do with wanting to achieve greatness in the classroom just as much as achieving greatness in sports.

"Intelligence without ambition is a bird without wings." – Salvador Dali

So when a lot of our young people enter the 9th grade and the realness of the classroom, education and learning hits them in the face, a lot of them will draw-back and won't even try anymore. Like in sports, the people that experience some kind of early academic success usually keep striving for more success.

I believe the scenarios I just described are natural reactions to circumstances, but there are some things that we can do to help bring about what we want in life.

It starts with parents. Most parents have the opportunity to instill love, self-worth, work ethic, discipline and more love in their children between the ages of zero to six years of age. This age range has been identified as the most important time to love, teach and discipline children. By six years old, children's personalities are in full swing, and it's very important to have something of value instilled within these young impressionable minds and personalities.

"Between birth and age 3, babies learn to give and receive love; to roll, crawl, stand, walk, and run; to talk, joke, rhyme, and sing."
- ZerotoThree.org

With this kind of effort and training from parents early on in the lives of their children, a lot of children and youth will ultimately develop the mindset of putting forth maximum effort in learning, sports and in everything that they do!

Expectations are a good thing. As a parent, educator and adult, we expect our young people to actually do certain things like being able to tie their shoe strings, clean up their rooms, dress themselves, etc., but it is our responsibility to teach them how to do the things that we want them to do. Never giving up, working smart and truly wanting to be the best, is a mindset of success.

YOU cannot afford to be LAZY!!!

Effort will separate us from at least 50% of our competition, and when we add a little bit of talent and the go-getter mindset, there is nothing that can stop you but YOU!!!

Our slogan at the "Make A Way" Education Program is "If you can't find a way … make a way!"

Play #2: Health (Alcohol, Drugs, Steroids & Sex)

*Definition of health (n) – Bing.com Dictionary

Health - [helth]

1. general physical condition: the general condition of the body or mind, especially in terms of the presence or absence of illnesses, injuries or impairments

2. overall condition of something: the general condition of something in terms of soundness, vitality and proper functioning

Are you keeping your body in tip-top shape? Are you one of those student-athletes that abuse their body and still believe they will be able to compete at a high level?

What you eat and how you eat (eating habits) are very important factors that determine the development of your mind and body. If you are below 18 years of age, there is a good chance that you are still growing. Why would you stunt your own growth? Of course there are exceptions to this age ceiling for people continuing to grow.

Are you drinking enough water every day? Are you getting the proper amount of rest every day (Eight hours are the recommended amount.)? Dehydration is a serious problem for a lot of people, and when dehydration reaches a critical point, it can easily be a fatal situation.

Our minds and bodies literally do not function well without the presence of the proper amount of water intake on a frequent basis. Drinking a certain amount of ounces per day that equals half of your body weight is a very healthy habit to start incorporating immediately. Eating the proper amount of fruits, vegetables, carbohydrates, protein, etc. contributes to amazing mind function and physical activity. Developing a meal plan that suits your lifestyle is important.

When you are a student-athlete experimenting or actually using alcohol and/or drugs, you may be setting yourself up for terrible things to happen such as drug addiction, drug overdose, failing drug tests, being kicked-off your team, expelled from school and being arrested. All of these consequences are negative.

I know a lot of young people believe that smoking weed (that "Loud") is cool, but it's not; and it can negatively impact your entire life. Check out this scenario:

You buy a dime bag of weed that has been laced with cocaine, roach repellent or another poisonous substance to give it some extra kick. You start smoking the weed and it does not connect with your system well. You start having convulsions, headaches, blurry vision and all kinds of different things happening to you that have irreversibly altered your mind, body or worse. You DIE! (i.e. Len Bias, University of Maryland; 1st Round Draft Pick of the Boston Celtics)

Does this sound like fun? No, I don't think so.

*Definition of steroid (n) – Bing.com Dictionary

ster·oid - [stéer òyd]

1. organic compound: any of a large group of natural or synthetic fatty substances containing four carbon rings, including the sex hormones

A lot of young people believe steroids will give them an advantage over their competition and it possibly may, but at what cost? You've seen the high profile cases of Lyle Alzado, Barry Bonds, Roger Clemens, Jose Canseco, Mark Mcguire, Rafael Palmeiro, etc. The personal embarrassment and disgrace alone is horrible, but steroids can affect your family, friends, teammates and school.

I'm one of the critics that say for steroids to really help an athlete, that athlete has to be very good already. Because the last time I checked, it still took amazing talent, skills, a tremendous amount of practice & dedication, plus a lot of good fortune to became a professional athlete. It's almost a dream to become an All-Pro, All-Star and Hall of Fame player.

Add in the possible health complications of using steroids, and it's a no brainer NOT to use them.

A very small amount of student-athletes get a chance to become professional athletes so you absolutely have to develop the right mindset and healthy lifestyle in order to create the life you want to live.

"Making the trip to professional sports is not an easy task and is only accomplished by a select few athletes. Determining how many college athletes go on to become professionals depends greatly on the sport. For example, in baseball, approximately 10.5% of college athletes make it to the professional world. However, only 1% of college basketball players go on to the NBA. About 2% of college football players make it to the NFL, while almost 6% are taken from high school into college football."

Reference: gcic.peachnet.edu

Your ability to learn, play sports and your life are not worth using drugs of any kind!

When it comes to sex, I know you have heard of the word abstinence, or at least I hope you have heard of the word abstinence.

*Definition of abstinence (n) – Bing.com Dictionary

ab·sti·nence - [ábstənənss]

>   1. self-denial: restraint from indulging a desire for something, e.g. alcohol or sexual relations

A lot of young people have been told to wait until they get married to have sex, and I actually agree with this philosophy because it will cut-down on a whole bunch of problems and situations that may arise from having sex before you are actually ready and responsible enough to have sex.

Believe it or not young people, we adults are not as naïve or clueless as you may believe we are about sex or any other topic for that matter … LOL …

When it comes to sex, a young man or woman needs to be aware of the consequences of having sex. The first thing you have to be aware of are your feelings. Are you feeling good or bad about yourself and the other person involved after having sex. The second thing you have to be aware of is contracting a sexually transmitted disease; including HIV. The third thing young people need to be aware of is that another life may be created. All three of these consequences are very serious and will affect you for the rest of your life.

STDs in Adolescents and Young Adults:

Public Health Impact

"Prevalence estimates suggest that young people aged 15–24 years acquire half of all new STDs1
 and that 1 in 4 sexually active adolescent females have an STD, such as chlamydia or human papillomavirus (HPV).2
Compared with older adults, sexually active adolescents aged 15–19 years and young adults aged 20–24 years are at higher risk of acquiring STDs for a combination of behavioral, biological, and cultural reasons. For some STDs, such as chlamydia, adolescent females may have increased susceptibility to infection because of increased cervical ectopy. The higher prevalence of

STDs among adolescents also may reflect multiple barriers to accessing quality STD prevention services, including lack of health insurance or ability to pay, lack of transportation, discomfort with facilities and services designed for adults, and concerns about confidentiality. Traditionally, intervention efforts have targeted individual-level factors associated with STD risk which do not address higher-level factors (e.g., peer norms and media influences) that may also influence behaviors.

Interventions for at-risk adolescents and young adults that address underlying aspects of the social and cultural conditions that affect sexual risk-taking behaviors are needed, as are strategies designed to improve the underlying social conditions themselves."

*Laboratory data is provided by the Center for Disease Detection, LLC; San Antonio, Texas.
- Special Focus Profiles: STDs in Adolescents and Young Adults
-STD Surveillance 2012

How do you focus on your class work when your emotions and feelings are all over the place? How do you focus at practice, the weight-room, film study and during the game when your mind is stuck on "gettin' some?" How do you tell your parents and coach that you need to go see a doctor because you are having some problems down there? How do you tell your favorite teacher, coaches, parents and family members that you are about to become a teenage mom or dad? Do you believe any of these consequences will alter your life plans? Of course they will.

Life is about choices and decisions. Let's learn how to make great choices and decisions; and then actually make great choices and decisions!

Your very life and the life of others may depend on it.

Play #3: High Performance in the classroom, at home and in the community

As a student-athlete, believe it or not, you are automatically under the microscope, and it's very important that you have your goals in place. If you have a list of timeline goals (short & long term) for yourself, they can actually keep your life on a positive and productive track.

Focus is the key to high performance! You wanting to be the best in everything that you do will ultimately lead to great results. Why? Because you will put forth maximum effort to achieve your goals!

In the classroom, are you satisfied with a "D" or "F" as your grade? You can't be satisfied! High performance in the classroom means your goal and standard is an "A" in all of your classes. Earning a "B" in a class is acceptable in most cases, but when a "C" is earned, that equals average. You cannot be happy with being average or mediocre. You must aim high to earn the very best result possible. That has to be your mindset and work ethic because even if you fall short of your goal, you will come very, very close to accomplishing what you set out to do.

How do you achieve high performance at home? I know that's the question you are pondering. It's a simple concept, but very difficult for children to do on a consistent basis. This even applies to our "Good Kids." You see, just like being on your sports team, you want to be coachable. Your parents don't want to keep asking you to clean up your room, take out the trash, wash the dishes, vacuum, cut-the-grass, do your homework, etc.

High performance at home means being respectful to your parents and your home; while at the same time respecting yourself and others.

That means when you go to school, you are continuing to do what you have done at home while achieving in school. How you act at home is usually just an extension of how you act in school.

High performance in the community involves community service, being involved in local events supporting great causes such as The Walk for Breast Cancer, The American Diabetes Association, The American Red Cross, your local library, church, synagogue or mosque, etc.

There are many ways to serve in your community and consistently deliver a high performance!

Play #4: High Performance on the field, court, track, mat, ice, etc.

High performance of the field is accomplished by being in tune with your mind and body. Are you willing to dig deep to be the best player at practice? Are you willing to be the best player in the weight room? Are you willing to be the best player during conditioning? Are you willing to be the best player during film study? Are you willing to be the best teammate ever?

All the questions I just asked will help you deliver high performances in your respective sport if you are willing to consistently do these things.

Most things in life are interrelated. There's a tremendous myth out here in the world that people, industries, etc. are independent. When the truth in most cases is that we are all dependent upon each other, and we all have to work together to make things happen no matter how big or small the task.

With that being said, let's look at how you can consistently deliver high performances for your team.

If you strive to be the best teammate, that means you will show up for meetings, practice and other organized team events on time and ready to go with a positive attitude.

If you strive to be the best player during film study, that means you have your notebook (paper) and pen/pencil ready for taking notes. It means that you are awake and alert listening to your coach breakdown your opponent, giving you technique clues and assessing your play.

If you strive to be the best player during conditioning and the weight room, you are properly rested and hydrated for each session. You are giving maximum effort during each drill, and you are providing encouragement to your teammates.

If you strive to be the player at practice, you are attentive during stretching, warm-up, drills and team play. You are moving full-speed with the intentions of getting better! Practicing is one thing, but practicing to get better takes you to another level.

When you attempt to practice perfect, you attempt to play perfect in games. That's when you see very high performances on game day!

The ability and effort to do this consistently is the key to becoming great, and it's applicable to everything you do in life!

"The will to win is not nearly as important as the will to prepare to win." – Bobby Knight (Legendary College Basketball Coach)

Play #5: Social Media & Technology

*Definition of Social Media (n) – Merriam-Webster.com

social media

forms of electronic communication (as Web sites for social networking and micro-blogging) through which users create online communities to share information, ideas, personal messages, and other content (as videos)

*Definition of technology (n) – Bing.com Dictionary

tech·nol·o·gy - [tek nóllǝjee]

1. application of tools and methods: the study, development, and application of devices, machines, and techniques for manufacturing and productive processes

2. method of applying technical knowledge: a method or methodology that applies technical knowledge or tools

3. machines and systems: machines, equipment, and systems considered as a unit

Not too long ago a person could feel very safe letting their guard down and just enjoying themselves without having to worry about someone taking a picture of them, video-taping them or recording their conversation. Now it's baaammm, got you! ... and it's all over Facebook, Twitter, Instagram, YouTube, Tumblr, etc.! Also, every day it seems like a young person is sharing a new messaging app with me (Snapchat, Kik, Vine, etc.). It is amazing how technology has advanced and given us tools that help us communicate and share information (good and bad) faster than ever before.

The good thing is that now it is much easier and faster to share pictures of loved ones with family and friends, but at the exact same time, it is amazing how this same technology may cause permanent damage to our reputations, careers, families and in some cases, literally our lives.

It is very hard to be one way at school and another way at home and in the community. You want to be as consistent as possible in living a positive lifestyle because not only is this a great way to live your life in general, but it allows you to be fairly insulated from social media attacks and other character issues that may arise.

If you are smoking, drinking, using drugs and philandering around in the community, there is a great chance that your principal, teachers and coaches already know from seeing posts online or being informed by someone else that has seen negative posts about you online.

If you are associated with known gang members or truly gang affiliated, how long do you really believe it will stay a secret? In most cases, things done in the dark will eventually be revealed in the light. Have you ever heard of Aaron Hernandez (former tight-end with the New England Patriots)?

So imagine college recruiters being very interested in you, and during the process of evaluating you, they do a social media check, and they find pictures and/or videos of you online drinking, smoking, throwing up gang signs and doing things that are not very flattering. What do you believe happens next? The recruiters stop calling, letters stop coming in the mail, etc. It's a wrap!

I truly understand that social media can be fun and wonderful, but it can also be damaging and cruel.

Let's learn how to manage our social media profiles and pages properly; and most importantly, let's conduct ourselves as outstanding people in all areas of our lives at all times so that we don't get caught slippin'!

I know it sounds tough, but I believe you can do it!

Play #6: Recruiting

When it comes down to recruiting, there are two major things you want to keep in mind and that's staying humble and being level-headed.

*Definition of humble (adj) – Bing.com Dictionary

hum·ble - [húmb'l]

1. modest: modest and unassuming in attitude and behavior

2. respectful: feeling or showing respect and deference toward other people

*Definition of Level-Headed (adj) – Merriam-Webster.com

lev·el·head·ed - \ˌle-vəl-ˈhe-dəd\

having or showing an ability to think clearly and to make good decisions

It is an honor for any school to want you to come be a student and an athlete at their respective institution of higher learning. There are only so many junior colleges, colleges and universities. For them to want to give you any type of scholarship to allow you to pursue your degree and to get a chance to play collegiate sports is an amazing opportunity!

As you continue on your journey of competitive sports, remember that you are a student first and an athlete second. When a recruiter visits your high school, they are looking at you in totality. Not just what you did on the field, court, track, mat, ice, etc. The first thing they look at are your grades, and if those are off track, they usually move on to the next player. Remember, there are more players than scholarship slots available. It's called "supply and demand" (Business education and economic classes teach you about this phrase.).

Let me share a great recruiting story with you. I had the pleasure of playing high school football with the #1 High School Wide Receiver in the country my senior year of high school. His name is Andre Hastings.

Prior to him becoming the #1 High School Wide Receiver in the country our senior year of high school, we met in the 8th grade, and soon became best friends by the time we were in the 9th grade. Fast forward to our sophomore (10th grade) year, and we ended up winning a Georgia 4A (The largest classification in GA at the time.) Football State Championship in 1987. We also finished ranked 19th in the country according to USA Today. We were rolling!

After we won the state title, we were getting ready for spring practice, and Andre was already receiving letters from colleges and universities during the spring of our sophomore year! Now, I didn't know anything about recruiting at the time, but I remember saying something like, "Dude, I don't believe there are too many 10th graders that caught 61 passes!" Right then and there, we verbally said that our goal was to earn scholarships to play college football.

As juniors, we had another impressive season, but we did not win another state title, we finished 9 – 3 losing in the second round of the playoffs (at that time, the region championship game). The most memorable part of my junior year was the fact that Andre and I were struggling a little bit in our Trigonometry class, and needed some help. One of our mutual best friends, Casey Gibson, a senior and headed to the Naval Academy; volunteered to tutor us in Trigonometry. Andre and I took education very seriously, and we knew the key to securing the scholarships we wanted were directly connected to our performance in the classroom just as much as our performance on the football field. So picture this, three starters from a state powerhouse high school football program were getting together after practice each day to improve in Trigonometry.

We are all great friends, brothers really, to this day, and I thank Casey for wanting to see his brothers improve and accomplish their goals!

During my sophomore year, I played on the junior varsity and varsity football teams. I ended up being the "Most Valuable Back" on the junior varsity team, and I played in two varsity games which included the State Championship Game where I had one carry for one yard ... lol ... What a thrill that was for a young 10th grader that was not expecting to play at all!

I earned a starting position as Free Safety going into my junior season, and I turned in a 2nd Team All-County performance that attracted me some attention. Add my football season to All-County, All-Region and County Player of the Year recognition in baseball; and I ended up receiving my first football recruiting letter in the spring of my junior year. All I remember thinking was, let's get this party started!

During my senior year, I literally remember seeing Lou Holtz, Dennis Erickson, Tom Osbourne, Ray Goff and plenty more big time division one head football coaches walking the halls of Morrow High School in Morrow, GA. They were there recruiting Andre, and it was beautiful witnessing it! One on the benefits of being Andre's best friend was when Sports

Illustrated visited the school to do an article on Andre, and we're being followed by a reporter and a camera man while walking around the school. They even attended one of our classes. It was truly a great experience! Reality TV coverage before reality TV. Where was Andy Cohen back then?

We finished 10 – 2 my senior year, and lost again in the second round of the playoffs (Yes, the region championship again. I still can't believe it!). We finished ranked number 7 in 4A for the State of Georgia, and even though I had another All-County, All-Region performance, being five feet, eight inches tall and 146 pounds, I didn't have any division one coaches beating down my door. But I did have a lot of division I – AA and division II coaches contacting me and coming to see me. I was very honored to have colleges and universities interested in me attending their schools and playing football, but I wanted to make sure that I got a quality education too. When my playing career was over with, I wanted to have a degree and the ability to get a job, start my own business or both.

I also had another great baseball season being named to the All-County and All-Region teams, so my senior year was a blast! I graduated with honors (top 5%), being the 18th ranked student out of 380+ graduating seniors!

After taking some college visits with my parents, and discussing my decision thoroughly, I signed my letter of intent to attend as a student and play college football at Presbyterian College in Clinton, SC on National Signing Day! A huge goal had been accomplished and an amazing dream realized! I graduated in four years and actually started my first business during my senior year of college.

Because of Andre's recruiting frenzy, he ended up signing two weeks later in a special news broadcasted event at his home where he decided to stay close to home and play college football at the University of Georgia! He also ended up being drafted in the third round of the NFL draft, and he had a very productive nine-year NFL career.

Here's the beautiful thing about our college careers. We both were Dean's List students!

Education and Athletics can take you very far in life if you keep both of them in perspective, and do your very best to be great in both of them. No one can ever take your education away from you, but at some point in time you will stop playing sports due to injury, age or desire.

With the right education, you will have the ability to learn, develop and master a profession, skill or trade that will allow you to be paid for your products and services over-and-over again via working for yourself and/or for someone else!!!

The Performance Pyramid

Play #7: College & Real Life

As I conclude this book, I want to make sure that I have expressed and emphasized how important it is for our young people to understand as soon as possible that education is directly connected to their earning potential.

As you are preparing to take the SAT and the ACT along with passing all of your "End of the Course Tests," you will also need to be researching the schools that best fit what you want to do in life. Do they have the major that you want to pursue, and what percentage of graduates gets jobs within the first six-months after graduation?

There is a commercial from the NCAA that tells everyone that Student-Athletes are more likely to go pro in a particular field of business versus going pro in their respective sports. With this being said, take full advantage of your college experience if you decide to go to college.

No matter which route you choose --- college or not, you have to prepare yourself to be a marketable and productive citizen that contributes to society. This can be accomplished by attending a trade and/or technical school along with enrolling in certification programs that are available.

The bottom line is being able to generate an income that will allow you to take care of yourself and a family when that time comes.

In most cases, high school is the only place that is going to treat you with kiddie gloves and allow you to get away with things you have no business doing. If you are naïve to this fact, college life and real life (when you are not allowed to go to high school anymore) are going to feel like running into a brick wall! You are going to probably say, "Why is everyone treating me this way?"

The reality is that once you graduate from high school or cannot attend high school any more, the world expects you to be able to do certain things, and be responsible for certain things. If you do not take your education seriously, and acquire at least the basic skills needed to move forward in life, then life can and will be very cruel to you.

Being a student-athlete is an awesome opportunity to take advantage of being a person that obtains and uses education to better themselves and others. It also allows you to be able to compete athletically at the highest level of a sport to represent a school, country and/or professional team. It's a privilege to be a student-athlete, and it means that you are held to a higher standard. Embrace the responsibility of being a student-athlete, and walk into your destiny with humbleness, level-headedness, pride and joy! One Love!

I BELIEVE IN YOU!!!

*Quotes from Current and Former Student-Athletes:

"A student athlete extends his or her talents beyond the boundaries of athletics."

LaTashae Walker, Ed.S
Student Athletic Program (SAP National)

"A Student Athlete is the nucleus of what sports are and what sports should be. Having the grades and the talent is just a testament to what being a well rounded player is and should be."

Cool Water – Former Basketball Player, Meadowdale High School; Dayton, OH
Alabama St. University Graduate (Montgomery, AL)
Rapper/Internet Marketer/Blogger/Consultant/Actor

"Being a student athlete is a blessing and a privilege. I experienced one of the greatest personal growth periods of my life thus far, and I will always cherish that experience. I became mentally and physically stronger; I learned perseverance and commitment; and as the captain, I learned how to be selfless and to put the team first. All of these are embedded in the success I've experienced in my life so far."

Portia Jones – Former Women's Basketball Player, Armstrong Atlantic State University
GA State Athletics (Student-Athlete Development)
Graduate Assistant- Football/Community Service

North Carolina High School Athletic Association

"A high school student athlete represents respect, responsibility and relationships. They have respect for their teachers, coaches, and peers. They are responsible for their actions on and off the court. And they build relationships with other athletes and students in their communities."
-*Ellie Caldwell*, North Henderson HS

"High school student athletes are the leaders and role-models for their community and peers. They possess the mindset to better themselves in all areas on and off the field and focus only on what is truly important in their lives to accomplish each goal they set."
-*Chris Ripberger*, Northern Guilford HS

"High school student athletes do not play sports for the glory. We go out and work hard every day because we have an internal desire to do our best. When we feel that we have reached our best, we push the threshold and work harder to reach the next level. There is no glory in high school athletics, but there is the internal satisfaction of achieving your goal, and that is better than any trophy."
-*Anna Broome*, Carrboro HS

"A student athlete is not only someone that represents excellence on the field and in the classroom; they are a prime example of leadership and responsibility."
-*Jordan Coley*, Mount Pleasant HS

"Student athletes exemplify the desirable qualities of leadership, teamwork, and determination in a grand balancing act while on the passionate pursuit of success."
-*Madison Maloney*, D.H. Conley HS

"Throughout my childhood I have grown up watching my grandfather be an athletic director and coach. I learned at an early age what an influence and role model athletes can be to their peers and to younger children. Win or Lose, athletes have the ability to be positive role models to those around them. As a student athlete now, I have to balance not only a hectic school schedule but also a busy sports schedule too. Hard work and determination may not always result in a win, but whether the outcome is a win or a loss, athletes are better people because they were part of the game."
-*Allyson Heath*, South Lenoir HS

Indiana High School Athletic Association Student Advisory Committee

"I believe that being a student athlete gives you the chance to not only be a part of a school but represent it. You are given the responsibility to put on a uniform and play for your team and your school, not just yourself. It's a very powerful opportunity, and I believe it can really define a person."
-*Kirsten Spangenberg*, Softball (Catcher)
Boone Grove High; Valparaiso, IN

"A high school student athlete includes both academic and athletic excellence. This excellence does not mean coming in 1st place or winning every game, but it means giving your BEST in all you do. A student-athlete also means being a student first and an athlete second. High school athletics are there to broaden different skills in the athlete's life."
-*Sara Slabaugh*, Cross-Country/Basketball/Track
Bremen High School; Bremen, IN

"Being a student athlete is learning to work hard and staying committed in all things you do. It teaches you that responsibility, dedication, and communication is key to success. A student athlete embodies leadership in the classroom, on the court, and in the community."
-*Olivia Gettelfinger*, Tennis (Varsity Doubles)
Bloomington High School North; Bloomington, IN

"I think being a student athlete shows what hard work and dedication can produce. Being a student athlete sets you at a higher standard than others. I believe that being a student athlete makes you a better person by learning valuable traits that are hard to obtain from other activities."
-*Jude Diagostino*, Football (Defensive Line/Linebacker)
Tri West Hendricks High School; Lizton, IN

"Being a high school athlete is an incredible experience. For me, it allows me to represent my school in a positive manner while doing what I love. It also allows me to become a more well-rounded individual. I have learned leadership, communication, and time management skills in my time as a high school student-athlete. I think being a student-athlete embodies hard work and determination to compete for your school and also for good grades in the classroom."
-*Turner Perkins*, Soccer
Danville Community High School; Danville, IN

"I believe being a student athlete is about learning life lessons while constructing friendships along the way. Perseverance, time management, resiliency and teamwork are just some of the skills acquired from sports that help drive you through life on and off the field."
-*Joel Boser*, Football
Hamilton Heights High School; Arcadia, IN

"As a student athlete, you must work hard and be organized. Playing a sport brings along many challenges, but also many rewards. It can teach a student many life skills like leadership and cooperation; and you must learn time management through juggling school work, games and practices. Being a student athlete prepares you for life beyond high school."
-*Lexi Place*, Tennis/Volleyball/Cheerleading

makeawaynow.com

*To secure Barry Brown a.k.a. B. Brown for Motivational Speaking, Appearances on Panels, Trainings and to order books in Team Sets ......

Please contact:

678.883.2734 --- Direct Business Line (Bar-Red Entertainment Group)

404.294.7165 --- Main Office (Hustle University & the "Make A Way" Education Program)

parentingyouthtoday@gmail.com

hustleuinc@gmail.com

B. Brown & Hotep at Northern Guilford High School with Student-Athlete Leaders after B. Brown's "Student-Athlete" Presentation!

Greensboro, NC

Made in the USA
Charleston, SC
23 June 2014